FROM
TO PLATE

A COLLECTION OF RECIPES
FROM MEMBERS OF
CHISWICK HORTICULTURAL
AND ALLOTMENTS SOCIETY

First published in the UK in 2014 by Chiswick Horticultural and Allotments Society, Registered Office: 5 Riverview Road, Chiswick, London W4 3QH

All proceeds from sales of this book go to Chiswick Horticultural and Allotments Society, Registered Charity No 1110134

ISBN 978-1-909105-05-8
Published on behalf of CHS by Pen, Plot and Pixel, 181 St Albans Avenue, Chiswick, London W4 5JT
Printed by West 4 Printers – www.west4printers.co.uk

INTRODUCTION

The idea for this cookbook came to us as we were serving up tea and cakes at one of our regular CHS Shows, and admiring the entries and the gorgeous donated cakes. We loved hearing people's recipes and the family stories that accompanied them and wanted to celebrate our shared enjoyment of growing and cooking with our own fresh produce, and the fellowship and fun we share with friends at the CHS as the society approaches its 100th Anniversary in 2015.

Vivien Cantor, Sue Gewanter, Jenny Jenks, Aileen Murphy, Penny Morris, Catherine Steele

ACKNOWLEDGMENTS

With thanks to the following who contributed recipes: Margaret Berger (MB), Daphne Boothby (DB), Nicola Callaghan (NC), Vivien Cantor (VC), Wendy Davis (WD), Denise Emslie (DeE), Diana Everett (DE), Sue Gewanter (SG), Elaine Hughes (EH), Jenny Jenks (JJ), Noreen Jones (NJ), Julia Langdon (JL), Lia Leonard (LL), Amy McElroy (AMcE), Pamela Mayorcas (PaM), Margaret Miles (MM), Jill Morris (JM), Penny Morris (PM), Aileen Murphy (AM), Diana Redfern (DR), Nathaniel Redfern (NMR), Norman Redfern (NR), Kay Senior (KS), Catherine Steele (CS), Frances Stonor Saunders (FSS), Cluny Wells (CW).

Also included are some recipes originally printed in CHS Handbooks, for entries to the Domestic Classes at the Summer and Autumn Shows.

Visit our website at www.chsw4.org

CONTENTS

CONVERSION CHARTS

When following a recipe, you should use either imperial or metric measurements, not mix them.

1oz	25g
4oz	125g
8oz	225g
12oz	350g
1lb	450g

1 teaspoonful (tsp)	5ml
1 dessertspoonful (dsp)	10ml
1 tablespoonful (tbs)	15ml

1 fl oz	25ml	
4 fl oz	120ml	
5 fl oz	150ml	¼ pt
10 fl oz	300ml	½ pt
15 fl oz	450ml	¾ pt
20 fl oz	600ml	1 pt

OVEN TEMPERATURES

°C	Fan °C	°F	Gas mark	Description
110	90	225	¼	Very cool
120	100	250	½	Very cool
140	120	275	1	Cool
150	130	300	2	Cool
160	140	325	3	Warm
180	160	350	4	Moderate
190	170	375	5	Moderately hot
200	180	400	6	Fairly hot
220	200	425	7	Hot
230	210	450	8	Very hot
240	220	475	9	Very hot

Note to Cooks

All the recipes in this book have been contributed by members of the CHS, their families and their friends, for you to enjoy. Not everyone supplied details such as how many people the recipe would serve, and some of the recipes are a little unspecific about quantities. Since we have not been able to test all of them, please use them with a small pinch of salt and forgive us if anything doesn't turn out quite as expected!

SOUPS

GranJan's Fennel Soup (NR)

This was one of my mother's favourite soup recipes and is now a family favourite, with or without the Pernod.

2 medium onions, finely chopped
2 tbs vegetable oil
2–3 heads of Florentine fennel (about 700g)
12 fl oz white stock (chicken or vegetable)
12 fl oz milk
Salt and pepper
5 fl oz single cream
2 tbs Pernod (optional)

Soften the onions in the oil, in a large pan, until they are translucent. Chop up the fennel, discarding any woody stalks. Add it to the onions and cook gently for a further 8–10 minutes, stirring occasionally.
Add the stock, milk and seasoning and then cover the pan and simmer gently for about 30 minutes, until the fennel is soft.
Using a stick blender liquidise until smooth (or transfer the soup to a liquidiser or food processor, whizz, then return to the pan).
Add the cream and Pernod and reheat very gently, then serve.

Simple Mushroom Soup (PM)

1 small onion, finely chopped
1 clove garlic, crushed
250g mushrooms, finely chopped
50g butter
2 tbs flour
900ml vegetable stock
500ml milk, or for a more luxurious texture, half milk, half double cream
Salt and pepper
Freshly grated nutmeg
Handful of chopped parsley

Gently fry the onion and garlic in the melted butter, until it is translucent. Add the mushrooms and fry for a further 5 minutes, stirring occasionally so the mushrooms start to exude liquid. Sprinkle the flour over the mixture and stir it in, cooking it for a couple of minutes. Add the stock and stir well, then simmer for about 15 minutes. Liquidise using a stick blender, or transfer to a food processor, whizz until smooth, then put back in the pan and add the milk, (and cream if using). Season, and add some grated nutmeg. Serve sprinkled with chopped parsley.

Butternut Squash Soup (NC)

2 medium size butternut squash
2 medium size onions
2 cloves of garlic
A splash of vegetable oil
A couple of sprigs of thyme
1 litre of stock (vegetable or chicken)
Salt and pepper

Peel, seed and roughly chop the squash into chunks. Peel and chop the onions, and crush the garlic. Put a small amount of oil into a large roasting tin and add in the squash, onions, garlic and sprigs of thyme.
Roast in a pre-heated oven for 30–40 minutes at 180°C / gas mark 4, or until all the ingredients are a nice caramelised colour, but not burnt.
Warm up the stock in a pan, and then put all of the roasted vegetables into a blender, with a couple of spoonfuls of the stock and liquidise. Return to the pan, mix with the rest of the stock and season with salt and pepper.
Serve with a nice wedge of crusty bread.

Lettuce Soup (PM)

This soup is a tasty way to use up a glut of lettuce or salad leaves from the allotment.

1 onion, finely chopped
1 oz butter
2 heads finely chopped lettuce
3 tbs flour
2 cups / ½ pt vegetable stock
1 cup / ¼ pt water
1 cup / ¼ pt milk
Salt and pepper
1 tsp paprika
Grated nutmeg (to taste)

Cook the onion in butter till soft. Add the lettuce and stir until it wilts, then stir in the flour, and then add the stock and water. Bring to the boil, then simmer for a few minutes, stirring. Liquidise using a stick blender in the pan or by transferring the soup to a food processor, whizzing it, then returning it to the pan. Add the milk, salt and pepper, paprika and nutmeg and reheat gently.

Carrot and Coriander Soup (NR)

500g carrots
1 onion
1 clove garlic
1 tbs vegetable oil
1 tsp ground coriander
1 litre vegetable stock
Plenty of fresh coriander
Squeeze of lemon juice
Grated nutmeg

Soften the carrots, onion and garlic in the oil, add ground coriander and cook for 1 minute.
Add the stock, and simmer until carrots are well cooked. Remove from the heat, add fresh coriander and blend until smooth. Add lemon juice and nutmeg, season to taste and serve. You could add a swirl of cream but it's healthier without.

Tomato, Carrot and Apple Soup (CS)

15g butter
2 tsp vegetable oil
1 onion, peeled and finely chopped
2 cloves garlic, peeled and finely chopped
175g carrots, peeled and finely chopped
450g tomatoes, skinned and roughly chopped
1 eating apple, peeled, cored and chopped
Bouquet garni
1.1 litres vegetable stock
Salt and ground black pepper

Heat the butter and oil in a large, heavy-based saucepan.
Add the onion and cook over a low heat until soft and
transparent. Add the carrot and stir over a low heat until
all the fat has been absorbed. Add the garlic, tomatoes,
apple, bouquet garni and stock. Season with salt and
pepper and bring to the boil. Cover and simmer for
45 minutes.
Remove the bouquet garni. Pass the soup through a fine
sieve or food mill. Return to a clean pan, heat through and
serve.

Borsch (CS)

350g whole, uncooked beetroot with leaves left on
2 large carrots
1 tbs vegetable oil
125g streaky bacon, without rinds and cut into small pieces
1 large onion, peeled and finely chopped
3 sticks celery, trimmed and cut in matchstick strips
1.4 litres vegetable stock
1 tbs red wine vinegar
Salt and ground black pepper
225g tomatoes
150ml sour cream

Wash the beetroot and leaves. Break off the leaves and separate them from their stalks and ribs. Cut the leaves into fine shreds and chop the stalks and ribs finely. Peel the beetroot and cut into thin strips. Peel the carrots and slice thinly lengthwise. Cut the slices into fine strips.
Heat the oil in a large, heavy-based saucepan, add the bacon and cook over a low heat until the fat runs. Add the beetroot, carrots, onion and celery and stir until the fat has been absorbed. Add the stock and vinegar and season with salt and pepper. Bring to the boil and simmer for 30 minutes.
Blanch and skin the tomatoes. Remove the cores and seeds. Pass the flesh through a fine sieve or food mill to make a puree. Add the puree to the soup with the beetroot leaves and stalks. Continue to simmer for

15 minutes or until the beetroot is tender. Serve with a swirl of sour cream in each bowl.

Watercress Soup (JJ)

40g butter
1 onion, finely chopped
1 large clove garlic, finely chopped
3 bunches of watercress, chopped (discard any thick stalks)
1.5 litres stock (vegetable or chicken)
Salt and pepper
Crème fraîche to swirl on top

Melt the butter in a large pan and soften the onion and garlic. Add the watercress and stir so it is coated with butter. Add the stock, salt and pepper and bring to the boil. Simmer for about 5 minutes. Taste for seasoning and add more if necessary. Remove from the heat and when cooled a little, liquidise either using a stick blender or in a food processor.
Serve in warm bowls with a swirl of crème fraîche on top.

Starters and Nibbles

Asparagus Tarts (JJ)

500g asparagus
120g crème fraîche
50g finely grated Gruyere
2 large egg yolks
1 tsp very finely chopped tarragon
Cayenne pepper
500g butter puff pastry, fresh or frozen
1 egg yolk plus 2 tsp milk to glaze pastry

Trim and cook asparagus in boiling salted water for 3–4 minutes, or until just tender. Drain under cold running water and pat dry.
Whisk together the crème fraîche, Gruyere, egg yolks, tarragon and a pinch of salt and cayenne, then chill.
Roll out the pastry about 3mm thick and cut into four rectangles 20cm x 12cm (or square if you prefer). With a sharp knife score the pastry 1cm around the edges, taking care not to cut right through. Place on a non-stick baking tray, prick the centres with a fork and chill for at least 30 minutes.
Heat the oven to 220°C / 200°C fan / gas mark 7. Divide the asparagus amongst the cases, laying side by side and trimming to fit. Spoon the crème fraîche mixture over the asparagus, chilled first so it isn't too runny. Brush the glaze over the exposed rims and bake for 15–20 minutes until golden.

Baba Ganoush (PM)

2 aubergines
1 red onion, finely chopped
2 tbs olive oil
1 tsp cumin powder
½ tsp chilli powder (depending on how hot you like it)
3–4 tbs of Greek yoghurt
Handful of chopped coriander leaves

Prick the aubergines, then put them under a hot grill, turning occasionally, until they are soft. Scoop out the insides into a sieve, discarding the skins. Chop the flesh up, and squeeze out as much liquid as you can. In a large frying pan, fry the red onion in the olive oil until it is soft. Add the spices and fry for another minute or two, then add the aubergines. Continue to fry gently for about 5–10 minutes, so the aubergine is soft and well mixed with the onion and spices. Add the coriander leaves and cook for another minute or two. Then mix with the yoghurt and spoon into a bowl. Serve with pitta bread. Nicest warm or at room temperature.

Mushroom and Watercress Pâté (PM)

50g flat mushrooms
125g watercress (about 2 bunches)
25g butter
1 medium onion, finely chopped
125g cream cheese
A few drops of Tabasco sauce

Finely chop the mushrooms and watercress. Melt the butter in a frying pan over a low heat, then add the onion and cook gently until soft. Raise the heat and add the mushrooms and cook briskly for about a minute, stirring all the time, then add the watercress and stir until it goes limp (takes about half a minute). Put all the contents of the pan into a blender with the cheese and Tabasco and whizz until you have a smooth pâté. It may take a few whizzes, with you stirring in the pate around the edges each time. Put into a pâté dish and chill until firm, then serve with hot toast.

Fritada (PaM)

This is 'fritada', nothing to do with the 'fritata' you may see in books of Spanish recipes or on Spanish menus. It is a Sephardi (Jewish) dish made from matzo meal, cheddar cheese, spinach and egg. It can be served as an appetiser, for 10-12 people, or as an hors d'oeuvre. The dish is less rich than the Greek spanakopita and less eggy than a quiche. To our family, it is the perfect food, and even better second time around, re-heated in a low oven.
As it is a very old family recipe it's difficult to give precise quantities.

4 or 5 bunches of fresh spinach or 4–6 bags of ready-washed spinach (frozen spinach can be used but defrost and squeeze out any excess water)
1 or 2 eggs
1lb cheddar cheese, grated
3–5 tbsps of medium Matzo meal (eg Rakusens, available from most supermarkets)
Black pepper
Small amount of butter or margarine

Preheat the oven, gas mark 4 / 180°C.
Wash the fresh spinach thoroughly and cut off any woody stems. Wilt the wet leaves quickly, with no added water, in a saucepan. Squeeze the spinach and pour off any excess water. If you are using frozen spinach there is need to cook it, just defrost and squeeze off any excess water.

Put the spinach in a large bowl. Mix in 1–2 eggs, (depending on quantity of spinach and size of eggs), and most of the grated cheddar cheese. Add couple of twists black pepper. Mix in several tablespoons of medium matzo meal, mixing well. The mixture should be dry, but not solid. Grease a shallow baking dish, tip in the mixture and spread it out with back of spoon, pressing it down — it should be about 15–20 mm thick. Sprinkle the remaining grated cheese over the top and a few dobs of butter or margarine. Bake in moderate oven for 15–20 minutes.

This dish is generally better cooked, cooled off, then reheated for serving the next day. As with many peasant dishes, it is remarkably tolerant of quantities, cooking temperatures and times.

As an alternative, which my family made for Pesach (Passover), sandwich the mixture between pieces of whole matzo biscuits.

Run whole matzos under tap so they are wet but not soaking. Place the matzos on greased greaseproof paper on a baking tray. Carefully spread the spinach mixture over, then top with second matzo. You may need to dob spoonfuls of the mixture rather than spreading it, to avoid cracking the matzos. Daub the top matzo with softened butter or margarine and sprinkling of grated cheese.

Bake in moderate oven, until tops are golden, about 15 minutes, but check that they are not getting too crisp and brown on top. Serve warm, cut into small squares. Both dishes can be frozen, wrapped in foil. Reheat with the foil opened up.

Mini Quiches (PM)

I perfected the art of making these little quiches in large quantities many years ago, when my then boss decided it would be more 'homely' if the staff did the catering for the annual Christmas Party (for around 120 guests and about 60 staff). I was one of the very few members of staff willing to cook and spent a happy day at home listening to Radio Four while making about 180 mini quiches, various salads, several cakes, a trifle, a lemon meringue pie, a chocolate mousse and some brownies. The guests were very complimentary about the food, but the following year we were allowed to use a caterer – I think the cost of all the ingredients, plus my taxi fare from Chiswick to EC2 transporting all the food, negated any saving the boss had expected to make by being 'homely'!

Shortcrust pastry (about 350g – I use a 375g packet of Jus-rol ready rolled if I'm in a hurry, but it puts the cost up)
1 courgette or about 6–8 mushrooms or 4 ripe medium size tomatoes and some basil leaves
¼ pt milk
2 eggs
Black pepper
Nutmeg
50g grated cheese (cheddar is fine, but other hard cheese works too)

Pre-heat the oven to 200°C / gas mark 6.

Grease a 12-hole bun tin with a bit of butter.

Roll out the pastry until it is about the thickness of a £1 coin or unroll if using ready rolled. Using an 8–10cm pastry cutter, cut out rounds to fit into the holes in the bun tin. Gently push the pastry discs down to fit snugly into the holes. Refrigerate while making the filling.

To make the filling, prepare the courgettes or mushrooms by chopping them into smallish chunks and sautéing them gently in a little oil or butter until softened. If using tomatoes, cut them into slices, removing the skins first if you prefer. Tear the basil leaves into small pieces.

Whisk together the eggs and milk in a jug and add pepper and a bit of nutmeg.

Take the pastry cases out of the fridge and put a little of the courgettes, mushrooms or tomatoes and basil into the bottom of each. Top with a pinch of grated cheese, then gently pour the egg and milk mixture into each case. Pop into the oven and bake for about 15 minutes, until lightly browned. After a couple of minutes, remove them from the tin onto a wire rack to cool.

These are great for parties as they can be made in advance and frozen, then defrosted and re-heated on the day.

Mushroom Pâté in Toastie Cases (DeE)

10 slices from a sliced wholemeal loaf
Butter for spreading

Set the oven to 220°C / gas mark 7.
Using a 6–8cm pastry cutter, cut as many rounds as you can from the slices of bread. If the bread is thick, it can help to flatten it with a rolling pin first. Spread the rounds thinly with butter or brush with a little olive oil, the press them firmly into small patty tins or individual bun tins, moulding the bread to the shape of the tin. Bake in the hot oven until golden brown and crisp (about 7–10 minutes). Remove from the tins and cool on a wire rack. They can then be topped with your choice of filling. The mushroom pâté below is very tasty.

1 small onion, finely chopped
250g mushrooms, chopped
25g butter
Cream cheese
Herbs, eg finely chopped tarragon or parsley

Melt the butter in a frying pan. Add the onion and sauté gently until translucent. Add the chopped mushrooms and continue to cook for about 10 minutes, until the mixture starts to dry out. Combine with the cream cheese and herbs, then spoon into the toastie cases. Serve warm or at room temperature.

Avocado & Green Pea Hummus (CW)

1 ripe avocado
30ml (2 tbs) lime juice
Half clove of garlic, peeled and crushed
300g can of tinned peas, drained (or equivalent of cooked frozen peas, cooled)
1 tsp Maldon salt
250g packet cocktail pumpernickel rounds or 30 thin slices of French bread, or 30 toastie cases (see previous recipe)

Spoon the flesh of the avocado into a food processor, add the lime juice and crushed garlic. Alternatively, mash them together in a bowl using a fork.
Add the peas and salt, then process again until you have a bright green puree.
Gently spread the pumpernickel rounds with the avocado and pea mixture. The purée can be made in advance and kept in the fridge, then spread on the bread or spoon into the toastie cases when you are ready to serve.

Cheese Straws (CS)

100g butter (plus extra for greasing)
150g mature cheddar or a mix of cheddar and Parmesan
100g plain flour (plus extra for dusting)
Cayenne pepper
Ground black pepper
1 egg yolk

Heat the oven to 220°C / gas mark 7. Lightly grease a large baking sheet and cover with baking parchment.
Finely grate the cheese into a mixing bowl. Sift in the flour. Add a sprinkling of cayenne and black pepper. Mix. Cut the butter into little cubes. Rub into the flour mixture. When crumbly, stir in the egg yolk using a round-bladed knife.
Gather the pastry into a ball. Dust a work surface with flour. Roll the dough into a rough square 5mm thick. Neaten the edges with your hands.
With a sharp knife, cut the square into strips and then each strip into fingers. Lift onto the baking sheet leaving space between the fingers.
Place in the oven and bake for 8 minutes checking after 5 or 6 minutes. They should be a pale, golden brown. Leave on the baking sheet for 5 minutes then lift the parchment onto a wire rack to cool.

Additional tips:
I use unsalted butter as I think the cheese is salty enough already. I use 100g cheddar and 50g Parmesan. The quantities for cayenne and black pepper depend on how "piquant" you want them. I use about ¼ teaspoon of each. I never bother greasing my baking sheets as they are nonstick and the parchment is enough.
Stick it all in a food processor and blitz until it comes together.
The space between the fingers is important. As they cook, the cheese melts and they do spread.
8 minutes is about right, even for a fan oven.

MAIN DISHES

Mark's Mum's Sausage Pie (PM)

I was born in Chiswick, but when I was eight my family moved to Yorkshire. My Chiswick-based grandmother told me all about 'the frozen north' and warned me that I would never be able to take off my vest, so I imagined it would be like living at the North Pole, but once there we were given a very warm Yorkshire welcome. This dish was cooked for us by the mum of my new friend Mark, and quickly became a family favourite (and still is).

1 large onion, chopped
1 tbs vegetable oil
450g tin of chopped tomatoes
8–10 skinless sausages, or equivalent veggie sausages
Quantity of mashed potato (approx. 3–4 large potatoes, mashed with butter and plenty of black pepper)

Gently fry the onion in the oil until it is soft then put it into the bottom of an oven-proof pie dish. Add the sausages to the pan and cook them until they are browned. Put the cooked sausages onto a chopping board or plate and cut each one into 3 or 4 chunks, then put them on top of the onion. Tip the tomatoes over them, spreading them out to cover the sausages. Add a dash of Worcestershire Sauce if you like. Top with mashed potatoes, then bake in the oven until the top is lightly browned. Serve with ketchup or brown sauce.

Andalousian Chicken (EH)

1 chicken (about 4lb)
1 large onion
Bouquet garni (or bunch of mixed herbs)
4 tbs butter
1 tbs olive oil
1 tsp salt
Freshly ground pepper
1 scant tbs plain flour
4 fl oz white wine
2 tbs tomato purée

Stuffing
4 oz boiled rice
4 oz cooked ham, diced
2 tsp paprika
1 tsp salt

Garnish
2 tbs oil
2 large onions, sliced into rings
2 large sweet peppers (de-seeded and de-stalked), sliced in rings
1 lb fresh tomatoes, peeled and chopped
1 tsp salt
Freshly ground black pepper to season

Mix the rice, ham, paprika and salt together and stuff the chicken with the mixture. Pin the neck flap neatly over the back with a small skewer. Heat the butter and oil in a heavy casserole pan. Lightly brown the chicken on all sides. Add the onion and the bouquet garni. Lower the heat, cover and cook for 1 hour at 200°C in the oven, or until the chicken is tender and the juices run clear from the thickest part.

While the chicken is cooking, make the garnish. Heat the oil in a pan and sauté the onions for 2–3 minutes. Add the peppers, tomatoes, salt and plenty of black pepper and cook gently until the vegetables are soft. Set aside, keeping the garnish hot.

Remove the chicken from the oven. Place the chicken in a heated serving dish, leaving the cooking juices in the casserole. Remove the skewer and surround the chicken with the vegetable garnish. Discard the onion and bouquet garni and place the casserole on a high heat. To make the sauce, sprinkle the flour into the casserole, stirring constantly with a wooden spoon. Stir in the tomato purée and the wine. Bring the sauce up to the boil, whisk to remove any lumps, then pour the sauce over the chicken and serve immediately.

Swiss Chicken (EH)

I was taught this recipe at the Chiswick Cordon Bleu Cookery School in 1973.

2½ lbs chicken breasts/leg portions

Giblet Stock
Giblets from 1 chicken
1 onion
1 carrot
Bouquet garni (or mixed herbs)
3oz unsalted butter
1 tbs chopped tarragon
Water

Sauce
2 oz unsalted butter
2 oz plain flour
¼ pt stock (see above)
½ pt single cream
½ pt dry white wine
2 oz Gruyere cheese or Emmental cheese (grated)
2 tsp French mustard (smooth)
Salt and pepper to season

Topping
4 tbs of toasted breadcrumbs
2 oz grated Cheddar cheese

Mix the butter and tarragon with seasoning and spread over the chicken portions. Roast for about 1 hour uncovered at 160°C / gas mark 3. Turn the chicken every 15 minutes and baste with the tarragon butter.

Make giblet stock by putting giblets, carrots, onion and herbs in a pan. Cover with ½ pint of water, and cook gently while the chicken is roasting. Take the stock off the heat and strain to remove giblets/vegetables. Put the stock in a jug.

To make the sauce, melt the butter, add the flour to the pan and mix to make a 'roux'. Off the heat, add the warm stock and use a whisk to remove any lumps until you have a smooth sauce, then add the cream. Bring the sauce to the simmering point, stirring with a wooden spoon all the time. When the sauce bubbles, add the wine and continue cooking for 5 minutes. Take off the heat and stir in the Swiss cheese and French mustard and season to taste. Cover and keep the sauce warm.

Remove the chicken from the roasting dish, reserving any tarragon butter that is left. Cut up the chicken into smaller portions. Using a gratin dish, coat the base with a little of the sauce. Put the cooked chicken pieces in the dish, drizzle the remaining tarragon butter on top of the chicken, then cover with the remaining sauce. Sprinkle with the toasted breadcrumbs and grated cheddar cheese.

Bake in the oven for 30 minutes at 180°C / gas mark 4.

Bobotie (JM)

A recipe originating from the Cape Malay people, this curried mince and dried fruit mixture is topped with a baked egg custard that has been spiked with fresh bay leaves. It is traditionally served with yellow rice. Serves 8.

2 onions, chopped
3 tbs sunflower oil
2 tbs paprika
2 tbs turmeric
2 tsp hot curry powder
2 tsp ground ginger
1 tsp cayenne pepper
2 tsp sugar
2 tsp salt
2 x 400g canned chopped tomatoes
125g raisins
110g tomato purée
4 tbs fruit chutney
2 tbs wine vinegar
2 tbs Worcestershire sauce
2 tbs apricot jam
3 slices bread, crusts removed and cubed
250 ml milk
2 kg beef mince
2 eggs, beaten
A few bay leaves

Sauté the onions in the oil in a large pan until they are soft and translucent. Add the spices, sugar and salt and cook for 2–3 minutes. Remove from the heat and add tomatoes, raisins, tomato purée, chutney, vinegar, Worcestershire sauce and jam. Return to the heat, bring to the boil and gently simmer for 2–3 minutes. Meanwhile soak bread in a little of the milk.

Add the minced meat to the onion and tomato mixture and mix thoroughly. Squeeze dry the bread, reserving the milk, and add to the mince mixture. Cook gently for 45–60 minutes stirring occasionally, until any excess liquid has evaporated. Adjust the seasoning of the mince mixture as necessary, then transfer to an ovenproof dish and smooth the surface. This dish freezes well — in which case stop here and freeze it. If using from frozen, defrost thoroughly, then continue as follows.

Preheat the oven to 180°C / gas mark 4. In a bowl beat the eggs and milk together then pour over the mince – it needs to cover the whole thing so you may need to tilt the dish. You are trying to achieve a thin layer of egg custard over the top. Decorate with bay leaves and cook in the oven for 15–20 minutes or until the custard has set.

Lamb and Leek Casserole (CS)

For the purposes of this story it is relevant to know that that my parents are divorced so visits to the family in the South West involve spending time with mother and father separately. On one such visit, we had lunch with mum where she served this casserole (that I had enjoyed as a child but forgotten) followed by her fabulous blackberry pudding.

That evening we went to dad's for dinner where he served... lamb and leek casserole followed by blackberry and apple crumble. So not only did we have to eat two meals in a day, we ate the same meal twice in a day. It's a good thing we like this recipe!

700g stewing lamb, cubed
50g plain flour
Salt and pepper
Vegetable oil
3 leeks, washed and sliced
400g tin tomatoes
275 ml stock
1 tbs tomato purée

Preheat the oven to 170°C / 325°F / gas mark 3.
Toss the lamb in the seasoned flour. Heat the oil in a frying pan and brown the lamb in batches. Remove to a casserole. Do not discard the seasoned flour as it will be needed later.

Fry the leeks until tender then add to the casserole with the tomatoes.

Stir the remaining seasoned flour into the fat in the frying pan and cook for one minute. Stir in the stock and tomato purée. Bring to the boil and add to the lamb and leeks in the casserole dish.

Cook in the oven for 2 hours.

Melanzane alla Parmigiana (AM)

900g aubergines, any colour or a mix
Salt
About 150ml olive oil
1 large red onion, peeled and finely chopped
1 garlic clove, peeled and finely chopped
1 quantity of fresh tomato sauce OR 600ml ready made
passata
115g freshly grated Parmesan cheese

Preheat the oven to gas mark 4 / 180°C.
Trim the aubergines and cut into lengthways slices about
2cm thick. Lay them in a colander, sprinkling with salt as
you go. Place the colander over a bowl to drain and leave
for about 30 minutes.
Heat 1 tablespoon of olive oil in a small heavy bottomed
pan and very gently fry the onion and garlic for about
15 minutes, until soft but not browned.
Once the aubergines are ready, rinse the salt off well, and
pat the slices dry with kitchen paper. In a large frying pan,
heat 2–3 tablespoons of olive oil and fry the aubergine
slices a few at a time. Repeat using the oil as needed, until
all the slices have been fried.
Add the cooked onion mixture to the tomato sauce and
spoon about one third of the mixture into a shallow 2 litre
oven-proof dish. Lay aubergine slices on top, then a
sprinkling of the cheese.

Continue to add layers of tomato, aubergines and cheese, finishing with cheese on the top.
Bake in the over for about 50 minutes, until golden and bubbling. Leave to stand for about 10 minutes before serving with a salad, and some crusty bread to mop up the sauce.

Bappa's Risotto (NR)

When he was in his mid 50s my father was sent to work in the Sud Tirol in northern Italy, where he and my mother then lived for 10 years. They loved the life there, especially the food and wine, and my dad became an expert at making risotto. This is his recipe.

1 small onion, finely chopped
100g butter
275g Arborio rice
Glass of dry white wine
1 litre vegetable stock, kept hot in a pan
50g Parmesan cheese, grated

Gently cook the onion in half the butter (50g) until it has softened and is translucent. Add the rice and stir so it becomes coated with the butter. Add the wine and cook until it has reduced by half, stirring all the time.
Add a ladleful of the hot stock and let the risotto simmer gently, stirring occasionally, until the stock has been absorbed into the rice. Add another ladleful or two, and continue in this way, slowly adding the hot stock until the rice has absorbed it all.
This will take about 25 minutes and is ready when the rice is tender but still has a little bite and the risotto has a creamy consistency. Stir in the remaining butter and Parmesan and serve immediately.

For 4 as a main dish or 8 as a starter.

You can add other vegetables to this, such as courgettes, asparagus, fennel, celery. Chop up your chosen vegetable, and add to the onions when they are soft, cooking for a few minutes before adding the rice. Also delicious if you add fresh herbs such as finely chopped parsley.

Tofu with Sweet Chilli Sauce (NMR)

1 packet of firm tofu, drained and cut into pieces (about 2cm x 3cm)
1 onion, sliced into chunks
4-6 small aubergines (or 1-2 large), cut into thick slices
3 tbs vegetable oil

For the sauce
250ml rice vinegar
125g white sugar
125ml water
3 tbs soy sauce
3 cloves garlic, minced
½–1 tbs dried crushed chilli flakes
1½ tbs cornflour dissolved in 3–4 tbs cool water

Make the sauce first, by placing all the sauce ingredients except the cornflour and water mixture in a saucepan and bringing it to the boil. Reduce the heat to medium and let it boil for 10 minutes, until it's a bit reduced. The vinegar may smell quite pungent as it burns off!
Reduce the heat to low and tip in the flour and water mixture. Stir to mix it in and continue stirring until the sauce thickens.
Remove from the heat and taste. If it isn't sweet enough, add a little more sugar. If it's not spicy enough for you, add a bit more chilli.

Heat up the oil in a wok, then tip in the chopped onion, tofu and aubergines. Stir fry for about 10 minutes, until the tofu is browned and the vegetables are cooked as you like them. Pour some sauce over the top and mix it in, and serve on a bed of sticky Thai rice.

You may have more sauce than you need, in which case it will keep in a jar in the fridge for a few days.

Tuscan Bean Stew (CS)

2 tbs olive oil
175g red onions, peeled and finely chopped
4 garlic cloves, peeled and crushed
2 tbs tomato purée
½ tsp chilli powder
125g carrots
4 tomatoes, skinned, deseeded and roughly chopped
2 sprigs thyme or a large pinch of dried thyme
2 bay leaves
Salt and pepper
450 ml vegetable stock
2 x 400g cans beans (such as butter, flageolet, kidney, chick peas) drained and rinsed
50g French beans, trimmed and cut into 1cm lengths

Heat the oil in a non-stick pan. Add the onions and cook for 10 minutes or until soft. Add the garlic, tomato purée and chilli powder and cook for 1–2 minutes.
Add the carrots, tomatoes, thyme and bay leaves. Season with salt and pepper. Pour in the stock then bring to the boil and simmer, stirring occasionally, for 20–30 minutes until the carrots are soft.
Add the canned beans and French beans then simmer for 5–10 minutes until the canned beans have heated through and the French beans are just tender.
Serve with crusty bread.

Fresh from the Garden

Fried Green Tomatoes (CS)

It's worth picking some tomatoes before they ripen, just to make this dish.

5 tbs olive oil
800g green tomatoes, quartered
3 garlic cloves, cut into small sticks
½ tsp chilli flakes
1 tsp ground cumin
Salt and pepper
1 tbs balsamic vinegar

Heat the olive oil in a wide frying pan and add the tomatoes, cut side down. Fry until browned on one cut side then turn to brown the second side. Add the garlic, scattering it between the tomatoes, with the chilli flakes and cumin. Allow the garlic to turn a light nut brown. Season with salt and pepper then add the balsamic vinegar. Serve hot from the pan or at room temperature with an extra pinch of chilli flakes on top.

Stir Fried Broad Beans with Thai Red Curry (CS)

900g fresh broad beans (unshelled) or 350g frozen broad beans
1 tbs groundnut oil
½ tsp ground black pepper
3 tbs finely sliced garlic
3 tbs finely sliced shallots
2 small red chillis, seeded and sliced
1 tsp sugar
2 tsp Thai red curry paste
1 tbs fish sauce or light soy sauce
2 tbs water

If using fresh broad beans, shell, then blanch them for 2 minutes in salted boiling water. Drain and refresh in cold water. When cool, remove the skins. If using frozen beans, simply allow them to thaw.
Heat a wok or large frying pan over high heat until it is hot. Add the oil and when that is very hot and slightly smoking, add the pepper, garlic, shallots and chillis. Stir and fry for 1 minute. Add the broad beans, sugar, curry paste, fish sauce and water and continue to stir-fry over high heat for 2 minutes. Serve at once.

Spicy Cucumber Salad (CS)

450g cucumbers
3 tbs fish sauce or light soy sauce
3 tbs lime juice
3 tbs water
2 tbs sugar
1 large fresh red chilli, seeded and finely sliced
3 tbs finely sliced shallots

Slice the cucumbers – unpeeled – in half lengthways and, using a teaspoon, remove the seeds. Then cut the cucumber halves into thin slices.
Combine the fish or soy sauce, lime juice, water and sugar in a bowl and stir until the sugar is dissolved. Add the cucumber, chilli and shallots and mix well.
Leave to marinade for at least 20 minutes before serving.

Runner Bean and Potato Curry (CS)

450g runner beans
2 medium potatoes
2 tbs vegetable oil
2 garlic cloves, crushed
1 tsp ground coriander
½ tsp ground turmeric
Up to ½ tsp cayenne or a chopped green chilli according to taste
1 tsp curry powder
½ tsp salt
¼ tsp garam masala

String the beans and cut into 1cm pieces. Peel the potatoes and cut into 1cm cubes. Rinse the potatoes and beans under a tap.
Heat the oil in a deep, non-stick pan (one which has a lid) and add the garlic, coriander, turmeric, cayenne or chilli, curry powder and salt. Stir for a few seconds and then add the rinsed vegetables. Mix well.
Cover and cook on a medium-low heat for about 15–20 minutes until done. It will cook its own steam so don't add any water. Mix in the garam masala and serve.

Continental-Style Red Cabbage (MB)

2 lb red cabbage, shredded and thick stems discarded
1 medium size onion, finely chopped
1 cooking apple, finely chopped
2 oz cooking oil
1 oz sultanas
2 oz brown sugar
½ tsp salt
¼ pint water
1 dsp caraway seeds
¼ pint vinegar

In a large saucepan put oil and onion, cook gently till the onion is soft. Add all the other ingredients and stir well. Cover with lid, bring to the boil and cook on low heat for 45 minutes, stirring occasionally. Add a little water if liquid is getting low. This can also be made in a pressure cooker, in 10 minutes.

Patatas Bravas (PM)

5 or 6 medium size potatoes (old are best)
Quantity of vegetable oil
1 tbs olive oil
1 small onion, finely chopped
1 clove garlic, crushed
Tin of chopped tomatoes
1 tbs tomato puree
1 tsp ground cumin
½ tsp chilli powder (depending on how spicy you like it)
Salt and black pepper

Peel the potatoes, cut them into small chunks and put them in a pan covered with cold water. Bring them to the boil, then simmer for 6 minutes. Drain and leave them to dry off for a few minutes.
Heat the olive oil in a heavy based pan, then add the chopped onion and garlic and gently sweat them for about 5–10 minutes, until soft but not coloured. Add the cumin and chilli and cook stirring for about a minute, then tip in the chopped tomatoes and stir in the tomato purée. Leave to cook for about half an hour, seasoning according to taste.
Heat the vegetable oil in a frying pan, then fry the cooked potato pieces until they are crisp and nicely browned. Put them in a warmed serving dish, with the tomato sauce on top. Serve at once.

Tomato and Fennel Salad (PM)

450g ripe tomatoes
2 medium heads of fennel
Sea salt and black pepper
4 tbs olive oil
½ tbs white wine vinegar

Skin the tomatoes scoring a cross in the bottom of each then plunge them into boiling water for a minute. Remove from the water, take of the skins and cut them into thin slices. Trim the coarse outer leaves from the fennel, then slice thinly. Arrange the tomatoes and fennel on a flat dish, season with black pepper and spoon the oil and vinegar over them. Leave to marinade for a minimum of half an hour, then add salt just before serving.

Serves 4–6 as a side dish.

Spanish Spinach (PM)

900g spinach, thoroughly washed
2 tbs olive oil
1 clove garlic
2 tbs pine kernels
1 tbs currants
Sea salt and black pepper

Cook the wet washed spinach in a pan, with no extra water, for about 5 minutes, or microwave for about 2 minutes, then put in a sieve to drain. When cool squeeze as much liquid out of it as you can, then chop finely. Heat the oil in a frying pan, then gently sauté the crushed garlic clove for a minute or two, being very careful not to let it brown. Add the pine kernels for a further minute, then the currants, stirring frequently, until they are all lightly toasted. Add the spinach and salt and pepper, and warm through, stirring well. Serve warm or at room temperature as a side dish or tapas plate.

A Glut of
Courgettes!

Courgette and Mint Soup (AM)

50g butter
2 medium onions, finely chopped
900g courgettes, roughly chopped into chunks
700ml vegetable stock
2 handfuls mint leaves, roughly chopped
Salt and pepper

In a large pan, melt the butter and add the chopped onions.
Fry them over a low heat until they are soft and translucent
(about 10 minutes). Add the chopped courgettes and fry
gently for another 5 minutes.
Add the stock and half the mint leaves, cover and simmer
for about 30 minutes, then allow to cool.
Add the remaining mint leaves, then either pour the soup
into a blender or food processor and or use a stick blender
in the pan and blend until smooth. Season to taste.
Then either warm up again and serve hot, or leave to cool
and serve at room temperature.
Serves 6.

Fried Courgette Flowers (FSS)

I have noticed many courgette flowers in the allotment are left to rot. One of my favourite recipes is battered courgette flower. The Italians do it in a deep fry batter but this is much simpler and easier to clean up afterwards.

Remove stamen and the small green pointy bits at the base of the flower. Beat an egg in a small bowl. Shake some plain flour onto a large plate.
Heat vegetable oil or olive oil in a frying pan, the more oil the deeper the fry, but half an inch depth should suffice.
Roll the flowers in the egg and then roll them in the flour until evenly covered.
When the oil is very hot, place the battered flowers in pan and turn gently to cook on each side.
Season with salt and pepper and serve – drain excess oil by placing them on kitchen roll before serving.

Courgette Bruschetta (AM)

4–6 small courgettes (about 700g)
4 tbs olive oil
2 cloves garlic, crushed
1 tbs shredded fresh basil
1 tbs shredded fresh parsley
½ tsp dried oregano
Salt and pepper
8 large thin slices of baguette or ciabatta, cut on the diagonal
80g hard cheese, thinly sliced

Preheat the oven to 200°C / gas mark 6.
Cut the courgettes into thin slices. Heat the oil in a large frying pan and cook the courgettes for about 10 minutes stirring occasionally and turning them so both sides get lightly browned.
While the courgettes are cooking, lightly toast both sides of the slices of bread.
Add the crushed garlic, basil, parsley and oregano to the courgettes, and season with salt and pepper. Cook for 2 more minutes, then remove from the heat.
Lay the toast onto a baking sheet then spoon the courgette mixture onto the slices. Cover with the sliced cheese and bake in the over until the cheese melts (about 4–6 minutes). Eat immediately.
Serves 4.

Courgette Frittata (AM)

1 tbs olive oil
4 medium courgettes, thinly sliced
1 red pepper, thinly sliced
1 or 2 cloves of garlic, finely chopped
6 eggs, lightly beaten
4 tbs sundried tomatoes, drained and chopped
2–3 spring onions, finely chopped
2 tbs fresh basil, or mint, or a mixture of both
Salt and pepper
25g of grated cheese such as cheddar

Heat the oil in a large frying pan and add the courgettes, pepper and garlic. Cook, stirring occasionally, for about 10 minutes, until they are soft.
Whisk the eggs in a bowl and add the sundried tomatoes, spring onions, herbs and seasoning and mix together. Reduce the heat under the pan and pour in the egg mixture, moving the vegetables around with a spatula so the egg runs under them. Cook over a low heat until the base is golden. Sprinkle cheese over the top and place the pan under a pre-heated grill until the cheese melts. Cut into wedges and serve immediately, with a green salad and crusty bread. Serves 6.

Very Easy Fried Courgettes (MM)

1 tbs olive oil
1 clove garlic, chopped
1 medium onion, chopped
2 or 3 medium courgettes

Soften the onions and garlic in the oil over a low heat. Finely slice the courgettes and add to the softened onion and garlic mix. Cook slowly, turning regularly until the courgettes are transparent. Add salt and pepper to taste and serve.

You can add other vegetables (eg peppers, tomatoes) or herbs eg parsley, chives, rosemary, thyme, marjoram to vary this dish.

Baked Courgette Casserole (AM)

About 1kg of courgettes, sliced
1 medium onion, thinly sliced
400g of tomatoes (fresh or tinned)
6 tbs olive oil
6 tbs vegetable stock
1 tsp brown sugar
2 garlic cloves, crushed
2 tbs chopped parsley
Salt and pepper
2 tbs bread crumbs
8–12 pitted black olives

Preheat the oven to 180°C / gas mark 4. Lightly grease a large casserole, then put a layer of courgettes in the bottom, followed by a layer of onion, then a layer of tomatoes. Continue to add layers until you have used up all the vegetables.
In a small bowl put 4 tablespoons of the olive oil, the stock, sugar, garlic, parsley and seasoning. Mix well and pour over the vegetables. Scatter the breadcrumbs and rest of the oil over the top. Bake in the oven for about 1 hour.
Garnish with the olives and serve with a green salad.
Serves 4–6.
This can be made using other vegetables, such as sliced new potatoes, aubergines, peppers. If you increase the amount of vegetables, remember to also increase the amount of stock.

Courgette Loaf (CS)

500g courgettes, grated
1 tbs oil, plus extra for greasing
8 spring onions, chopped
1 garlic clove, crushed
250g Cheddar cheese, grated
150ml sour cream
4 eggs, separated
50g fresh breadcrumbs
25g ground almonds
Salt and pepper

Put the courgettes in a sieve, sprinkle with salt and leave for 30 minutes. Rinse and pat dry.
Grease and line a 20cm round cake tin. Preheat the oven to 160°C / gas mark 3.
Heat the oil and fry the spring onions and garlic until soft. Transfer to a bowl and mix in the courgettes, cheese, sour cream, salt and pepper. Stir in the egg yolks, breadcrumbs and almonds. Whisk the egg whites until stiff and fold into the courgette mixture. Spoon into the tin and bake for one hour until golden. Serve warm or cold, cut into wedges.

Courgette, Tomato and Brie Tart (CS)

1 pack ready rolled puff pastry
2 tbs tomato purée
200g Brie
4–5 largish ripe tomatoes
200g courgettes
1 tsp dried oregano
2 tsp olive oil
Salt and pepper

Preheat the oven to 200°C / 180°C fan / gas mark 6.
Run water over a baking sheet, shake off the excess then put the pastry on the sheet. Mark around the pastry with a knife about 20cm from the edges. Prick the pastry base with a fork, keeping inside the marks. Spread the tomato purée over the pastry base. Cut the Brie into long, thin slices. Cut the tomatoes and courgettes into thin slices. Heat the olive oil in a frying pan and fry the courgettes for one to two minutes until softened. Add the oregano and season with salt and pepper. Cook for a further one to two minutes then allow to cool slightly.
Starting from one short end of the pastry base, arrange overlapping rows of Brie, tomatoes and courgettes within the cut marks. Brush or drizzle over the pan juices and season. Bake in the oven for 25 to 30 minutes until the pastry is puffed up and the courgettes are tender. Serve warm.

More Very Easy Fried Courgettes (DB)

Harvest the courgettes when they reach about 15 cms in length.
Top and tail then slice lengthwise (about ½ cm thick).
Lay out on a large plate and pour on a little olive oil.
Sprinkle on a little brown sugar, some chopped garlic and a twist of pepper.
Leave to marinate for about half an hour.
Heat a griddle pan (one with bars) then lay the courgette slices on it, sugared side down and allow to brown but not burn. Flip over in the pan, and cook for a further minute or two, then serve with the grilled stripes showing.

Even More Very Easy Fried Courgettes! (DB)

Chop courgettes into cubes (about 2cm) or slice into rings.
Put into a frying pan together with crushed garlic and a generous amount of chopped parsley.
Pour over a little olive oil and gently fry to a light golden brown and serve.

The Beaut Aussie Zucchini Slice (JL)

My fellow allotmenteer often has an excess of courgettes in the autumn so I sent her this recipe that our family call 'The Beaut Aussie Zucchini Slice'. Lovely Australian Kate wrote it into my recipe file under this title when the children were small. It works unfailingly and is endlessly adaptable. It also briefly succeeded in beguiling children who thought they didn't like courgettes into eating zucchini, which they have since always loved. It's also easy to make two small dishes at the same time, one without meat, if you have a vegetarian in the family, although my mother famously once made it for my vegetarian daughter who looked up from her meal and asked, 'Granny does this have bacon in it?' My mother blushed very slightly and said, 'Only a little streaky, darling, for the flavour...'
Good hot, warm or cold.

375g courgettes, washed and topped and tailed
1 large onion, finely chopped
3 bacon rashers or a couple of slices of ham, chopped up (optional, depending on whether you are making a veggie version)
5 eggs
80g grated cheddar cheese
150g self-raising flour
125 ml oil
Salt and pepper
Sunflower seeds (optional)

Grate unpeeled courgettes coarsely. Lightly beat the eggs in a bowl, then add all the other ingredients. Pour into well-greased dish and bake in moderate oven for 30–40 minutes until nicely browned. If using sunflower seeds, sprinkle over the top before baking.

This seems to work with any proportions and of course can be widely adapted with other cheeses, herbs, nuts, chorizo and so on.

PUDDINGS AND DESSERTS

Rhubarb Sorbet (MM)

500g rhubarb
225g caster sugar
Juice of 1 lemon
150ml water

Wash, trim and cut the rhubarb into 2 cm chunks. Place the rhubarb, sugar, lemon juice and water in a pan and gently cook until soft, around 15–20 minutes. Allow rhubarb to cool then blend mixture in a liquidiser until smooth. Freeze in an airtight container, stirring every hour to prevent ice crystals forming, until set, (around 4–6 hours).
Alternatively use an ice cream maker to churn, then store in an airtight container and freeze for around 4 hours until set.
When serving, remove from the freezer about 20–30 minutes before you want to eat it, to allow it to soften.

Easy Peasy Trifle
(AM with thanks to Peter Robinson)

Packet of madeleines or boudoir biscuits
Bottle of green ginger wine
Double cream, lightly whipped until it has thickened
Icing sugar
2 packets of ready to eat passion fruit, or other prepared
fruit eg pineapple

Break up the madeleines or boudoir biscuits and put them
in a bowl. Pour over the ginger wine to moisten the
sponges. Lightly whip the double cream until it has
thickened, adding the icing sugar as you do it.
Break up the passion fruit, (reserving a few for decoration)
and mix with the cream and sugar. Spoon the cream
mixture onto the madeleines. Scatter the remaining fruit
on the top.

Di's Raspberry Trifle (PM)

Packet of trifle sponges
Raspberry jam
Orange juice (about 5 fl oz)
225g (or thereabouts) fresh raspberries
Pack of instant custard
10 fl oz fresh double cream
Small piece of dark chocolate

Cut the trifle sponges into quarters, and in half horizontally. Spread a little raspberry jam onto half the pieces and sandwich them together with the rest of the pieces. Put the sponges 'sandwiches' into the bottom of a trifle dish or bowl. Sprinkle orange juice over the top of the sponges, so they become moist (but not soggy). Tip in the raspberries, mix them into the sponge pieces and level the mixture off. Pour the custard over the mixture, levelling it off. Refrigerate, so the custard can firm up. Whip the double cream until it is thick, then spoon it gently over the custard, to cover the top of the trifle. Grate a little dark chocolate on top, for decoration. Refrigerate until you eat it.

Amy's LA Cheesecake (AMcE)

220g digestive biscuits, crushed into small crumbs
½ tsp cinnamon powder
110g unsalted butter, melted
500g cream cheese
3 eggs
200g caster sugar
550ml sour cream
Zest from 1 lemon
1tsp vanilla essence

Preheat the oven to 160°C / gas mark 3.
Lightly butter the bottom and inside edges of a 20cm
spring-form cake tin. Mix the digestive biscuit crumbs,
cinnamon and melted butter, then put them in the cake tin,
pressing them down to cover the bottom and up the sides.
Refrigerate.
Using an electric mixer, beat the cream cheese for about a
minute until it is smooth, then add the eggs, one at a time,
and continue to beat until combined. Gradually add the
sugar, continuing to beat for 1–2 minutes.
Add the sour cream, lemon zest and vanilla essence,
beating again, but don't overbeat, just combine thoroughly.
Pour the filling on top of the biscuit crumb base and
smooth with a knife.
Set the cake tin on top of a sheet of aluminium foil and
bring the foil up the sides of the tin, to make it watertight.
Put the wrapped tin into a large baking tray, then pour

boiling water into the baking tray, to come about half way up the side of the cake tin. Bake in the oven for about an hour. It may take a bit longer than this, but be careful not to overcook – the cheesecake should still jiggle a bit in the centre when taken out, as it will firm up when cold. Leave it to cool in the baking tray for about 30 minutes, then lift out, and chill in the refrigerator for at least 4 hours. Then run a thin knife around the edge and remove the spring-form ring. Serve with fresh fruit.

Yogi Pud (NR)

This was one of my mum's recipes that she often made when we were children. She would use various flavours of yoghurt, though we always preferred strawberry. It works best if the mixture is at room temperature when the gelatine is added.

4 x 10 ml cartons of yoghurt, all the same flavour
¼ pint of double cream
4 tbs caster sugar
½ oz gelatine or vegetarian equivalent (vegi-gel), dissolved in 2 tbs warm water

Whip the cream lightly, until it thickens. Beat in the yoghurt and sugar. Mix in the dissolved gelatine and water, then pour into a serving dish and leave it to set. Serve with fresh fruit that complements the yoghurt flavour.

Granpa Norm's Chocolate Sauce (WD)

My father-in-law, Norm Davis, was a professional chef and as a young man was one of the pastry chefs working at Buckingham Palace at the time of the Queen's Coronation. He went on to become an HMI food inspector, but never lost his touch with cakes and pastries, and when I married his son, my mum made the wedding cake and Norm did the icing. We didn't want a traditional white cake so he made the icing using whisky, which made it a lovely golden colour.

This sauce is fabulous hot on top of pears and vanilla ice cream. It also goes very well with profiteroles.

2 oz cocoa powder
2 oz butter
4 oz caster sugar
Drop of vanilla essence
4 dsp of hot water

Mix all the ingredients together in the top of a double boiler, or in a bowl over hot water, until the butter has melted, the cocoa has cooked a bit and everything is well combined. Serve hot. Can be kept in the fridge for a day or two and gently reheated.

Buttermilk Pudding (JJ)

Makes 10 generous portions – it is delicious but very rich, so halve the quantities if necessary.

4 leaves (8g) gelatine
500ml double cream
140g sugar (or less to your taste)
1 vanilla pod
500ml buttermilk
½ lemon, juiced

Soak the gelatine leaves in cold water for 5 minutes.
Put the double cream, sugar and vanilla pod in a pan. Boil for 1 minute then remove from the heat.
Drain the gelatine and add to the cream mix, stir well, pass through a fine sieve and leave to cool down.
When the mixture is around 35°C (still warm but not beginning to set) add the buttermilk and lemon juice, stir well, then pour into the desired mould or moulds.

Tiramisu (CS)

3 eggs, separated
450g mascarpone cheese
2 tsp vanilla sugar
175ml very strong black coffee
120ml coffee liqueur
18 savoiardi (Italian sponge fingers)
Sifted cocoa powder and grated bittersweet chocolate to finish

Put the egg whites in a grease free bowl and whisk with an electric mixer until stiff and in peaks.
Mix the mascarpone, vanilla sugar and egg yolks in a separate large bowl and mix with the electric mixer until evenly combined. Fold in the egg whites then put a few spoonfuls of the mixture in the bottom of a large serving bowl and spread it out evenly.
Mix the coffee and liqueur together in a shallow dish. Dip a sponge finger in the mixture, turn it quickly so that it becomes saturated but does not disintegrate then place it on top of the mascarpone mixture in the serving bowl. Add five more dipped sponge fingers, placing them side by side. Spoon in about one third of the remaining mascarpone mixture and spread it out. Make more layers in the same way, ending with mascarpone. Level the surface. Cover and chill overnight. Sift the cocoa powder over the top and sprinkle with grated chocolate before serving.

Simple Chocolate Mousse (PM)

200g plain chocolate
4 eggs
2 tbs rum (optional)

Melt the chocolate in a bowl over hot water. Separate the egg whites from the yolks, being very careful not to get even the tiniest bit of yolk in the white.
When the chocolate has melted, but cooled a little, beat the eggs yolks into the chocolate – it will go very stiff to begin with, but keep beating until it gets smooth again. If you like, add a couple of tablespoons of rum at this point. In a very clean bowl, whisk the egg whites until they are stiff. Gently fold the egg whites into the chocolate mixture using a metal spoon, combining it well. Pour into a serving dish and refrigerate until firm (at least a hour, preferably longer).

Serves 4. If you want to change the quantities, just decrease or increase on the basis of 50g of chocolate and 1 egg per person.

Wickedly Delicious Chocolate Cake (PM)

400g plain chocolate
225g soft margarine
100g icing sugar
5 eggs, separated
2 tbs plain flour
Butter for greasing the cake tin

Turn on the oven to gas mark 4 / 180°C.
Grease a cake tin of around 20 cm in diameter. If it doesn't
have a loose bottom, line the bottom with buttered
greaseproof paper.
Melt the chocolate in a large bowl over a pan of hot water,
stirring only once or twice, then leave to cool down. Using
an electric mixer, cream the margarine and icing sugar
together, then beat in the egg yolks. Then stir in the melted
chocolate gently using a metal spoon (not a beater), then
stir in the flour. In a clean bowl, whisk the egg whites until
they are firm enough to stand in peaks. Gently fold the egg
whites into the chocolate mixture, then pour the mixture
into the cake tin. Put it in the pre-heated oven for about
45 minutes. The top should start to crack a little. No point
in testing with a skewer as even when it's ready, it will still
be moist in the middle. Take it out of the oven and leave it
to cool in the tin, then remove from the tin and leave to
cool further on a wire rack. Serve in small slices (as it is very
rich), with a dollop of thick cream or crème fraîche.

BREAD, CAKES, BISCUITS AND COOKIES

The Queen Mother's Cake (VC)

This is believed to have been the Queen Mother's favourite cake. She decreed that the recipe should only be used for charitable purposes.

Pour one breakfast cup (10 fl oz / ½ pt) of boiling water over 8 oz of chopped dates and add one teaspoon of bicarbonate of soda. Let this stand for the time it takes to mix the following:

8 oz sugar
8 oz butter
1 beaten egg
1 tsp baking powder
1 tsp salt
1 tsp vanilla
2 oz chopped walnuts
10 oz plain flour

Once mixed, add all the above to the date mixture and bake for 35 minutes in a moderate oven in 9"x 12" cake tin.

Topping:
5 tbs brown sugar
2 tbs butter
2 tbs cream

Mix these ingredients together in a pan and gently boil for 3 minutes stirring all the time. Be careful not to boil this mixture for any longer or it will turn to toffee! It should have the consistency of fudge.

Spread the topping onto the cake and sprinkle with chopped nuts.

Irish Brack (AM)

500g mixed dried fruit
200g soft brown sugar
300ml cold tea
1 egg, beaten
275g self-raising flour

Put the fruit, sugar and tea in a bowl, and leave for about 3 hours, until the tea has been absorbed. Line and grease a 1 kg loaf tin. Preheat the oven gas mark 4 / 180°C.
Beat the egg and flour into the fruit and sugar mixture, then spoon the mixture into the loaf tin. Bake in the oven for about 1½ to 1¾ hours.
Leave in the tin for about 5 minutes, then take out and cool on a wire rack. Serve with butter.
Makes a 1 kg loaf.

Cake Salé/Savoury Bread (SG)

This is called Cake Salé or Savoury Bread and is from the Belmont Primary School Cook Book produced in 2003. It's very easy and very delicious!

You can easily make it vegetarian by omitting the bacon or ham.

2 eggs
Salt
100 ml white wine
100 ml olive oil
225g self-raising flour
100-150g grated cheese (even supermarket reduced-fat grated cheese works well!)
Optional additions; chopped garlic, chopped bacon/diced ham, chopped olives, herbs and sautéed onion (I've also added cherry tomatoes – very nice)

Preheat the oven to 200°C / 400°F / gas mark 6. Grease a roasting tin measuring approximately 30 x 20 cm.
Mix the eggs, a pinch of salt, white wine and oil together.
Sift the flour into a large bowl, making a well in the centre and add the liquid ingredients gradually, beating well to get rid of any lumps.

Add the cheese, garlic, bacon, olives, etc, as you prefer. The mixture should not be too thick – if so, add a little more wine.

Pour it into the prepared tin, make sure it is level and cook in the preheated oven for approximately 35 minutes or until it looks cooked and golden brown and a knife comes out clean when pushed into the centre. Serve warm.

Carrot and Orange Squares
(CHS Summer Show 2013)

250ml sunflower oil
225g caster sugar
3 large eggs
225g self raising flour, pinch of salt
250g grated carrot.

For the icing:
50g unsalted butter
200g cream cheese
40g icing sugar, sifted
Finely grated rind of 2 oranges
2 tbs orange juice

Preheat the oven to 180°C / 160°C fan oven / gas mark 4. Grease with butter and baseline an 18cm x 28cm, 2½cm deep, tin. Whisk the oil and sugar together, then whisk in the eggs one at a time. Gently fold the flour and salt into the mixture, then fold in the grated carrot. Pour into the tin and bake for 40 minutes, until golden and a skewer inserted in the centre comes out clean. Leave in the tin for 10 minutes, then turn onto a wire rack.

For the icing, beat together the butter and cream cheese until light and fluffy. Beat in the icing sugar, half the orange rind and juice. When the cake is cold, remove the lining

paper, cover with a 5mm layer of icing and decorate with the remaining orange rind.
Cut into 12 squares to serve.

Chocolate Brownies
(CHS Autumn Show 2013)

100g unsalted butter
200g dark chocolate, chopped up
4 eggs
250g golden caster sugar
100g plain flour
1 tsp baking powder
30g cocoa powder

Heat the oven to 180°C / fan oven 160°C / gas mark 4. Line a 22cm square brownie tin with baking parchment. Melt the butter and chocolate together in a microwave or in a bowl set over a pan of simmering water. Cool to room temperature. Whisk the eggs and sugar together until the mixture is light and fluffy. Fold the chocolate mixture into the egg mixture, then sift in the flour, baking powder and cocoa. Fold this in to give a fudgy batter and pour it into the tin, levelling it off. Bake for 25–30 minutes or until the top is starting to crack and the middle is set. Cool completely, then turn out of the tin and cut into 12 pieces.

Lemon Drizzle Cake
(CHS Summer Show 2012)

225g unsalted butter, softened
225g caster sugar
4 eggs
225g self-raising flour
Finely grated zest 1 lemon

For the drizzle topping:
Juice 1½ lemon
85g caster sugar

Preheat the oven to 180°C / fan oven 160°C / gas mark 4.
Line a 1kg loaf tin (8cm x 21cm) with greaseproof paper.
Beat together the butter and sugar until pale and creamy,
then add the eggs, one at a time, slowly mixing through.
Sift in the flour and add the lemon zest and mix until well
combined.
Spoon the mixture into the prepared tin and level the top
with a spoon. Bake for 45–50 minutes until a thin skewer
inserted into the centre of the cake comes out clean.
While the cake is cooling in its tin, mix together the lemon
juice and sugar to make the drizzle topping. Prick the
warm cake all over with a skewer or fork then pour over
the drizzle – the juice will sink in and the sugar will form a
crisp topping. Leave in the tin until completely cool.

Gingerbread
(CHS Autumn Show 2012)

100g unsalted butter
200g black treacle
150ml milk
200g plain flour
1 tsp mixed spice
2 tsp ground ginger
1 tsp bicarbonate of soda (baking powder)
50g soft dark brown sugar
2 eggs

Preheat the oven to 150°C / gas mark 2. Line an 18cm square baking tin with greaseproof paper.
Warm the butter and treacle together. Add the milk and allow to cool. Sift the flour, mixed spice, ginger and bicarbonate of soda into a bowl. Add the treacle mixture, sugar and eggs. Beat well.
Spoon the mixture into the prepared tin and bake for 1¼ to 1½ hours until firm to the touch. Cool in the tin, then cut into slices.

Lia's Lemon Drizzle Cake (LL)

320g caster sugar
3 eggs
Grated zest of 2 lemons
350g plain flour
1 tsp salt
1½ tsp baking powder
250 ml milk
1 tsp vanilla extract
200g melted butter or margarine

For the drizzle:
Juice and zest of 1 lemon
50g caster sugar
100 ml water

Preheat oven to 180°C / gas mark 4.
Grease and line with baking parchment a 25cm square cake tin or 25cm diameter spring-form tin.
In a large bowl, combine sugar, eggs and lemon zest. Mix well, either with a wooden spoon or with an electric mixer. Sift in the salt, baking powder and half of the flour, plus the milk and vanilla extract. Mix well. Sift in the rest of the flour and stir again until the mixture is light and fluffy.
Now pour in the melted butter and mix gently until thoroughly combined. Pour the mixture into the prepared cake tin and bake for about 45–50 minutes until the cake is golden brown and bounces back when touched.

When the cake is nearly ready, make the lemon drizzle. Put lemon juice and zest, sugar and water in a small saucepan. Slowly bring to a boil, then simmer until liquid is reduced by half and is a bit syrupy. When the hot cake comes out of the oven, pour the drizzle on top. Leave the cake to cool slightly in the tin before turning out to cool completely on a wire rack.

Traditional Chocolate Chip Cookies (AMcE)

150g salted butter, softened
80g dark brown sugar
80g granulated sugar
2 tsp vanilla extract
1 large egg
225g plain flour
½ tsp bicarbonate of soda
¼ tsp salt
150g chocolate chips or chunks

Preheat the oven to 190°C / gas mark 5.
Line two baking trays with non-stick paper. Put the softened butter and the sugars into a bowl and beat until creamy. Add the vanilla essence and egg and beat again. Sift in the flour, bicarbonate of soda and salt and beat again. Stir in the chocolate chips.
Using a teaspoon put small amounts of the mixture on the baking trays, keeping them well apart as the mixture will spread when it cooks. Bake in the oven for 8–10 minutes, until lightly browned round the edges but still soft in the centre. Leave on the trays for a few minutes to firm up then transfer to a wire rack to cool. These will keep well in a tin for a few days (if you can resist!)

Apple Buns (NR)

8 oz plain flour
1 tsp cream of tartar
½ tsp bicarbonate of soda
Pinch of salt
4 oz butter
4 oz caster sugar
1 egg
1 cup stewed apple

Preheat the oven to gas mark 6 / 200°C.
Mix the flour, cream of tartar, bicarbonate of soda and salt, then rub the butter into the dry ingredients until it looks like breadcrumbs. Stir in the sugar, then mix with the egg to bind to a soft dough.
Roll out the dough on a very lightly floured board, and cut out twelve rounds using a 2 inch pastry cutter. Put the rounds into lightly greased buns tins, pressing them down to make little cups. Put a teaspoonful of stewed apple into each cup.
Pull together the remaining pastry and re-roll it, then cut twelve 1½ inch rounds to use as lids. Press the lids onto the bottoms, sealing in the apple.
Cook in a hottish oven for 15 minutes, then cool on a wire rack.

Sticky Almond Cake (VC)

225g (8oz) butter
225g (8oz) caster sugar
4 eggs beaten
50g (2oz) plain flour
175g (6oz) ground almonds
½ teaspoon almond essence
350g (12oz) white marzipan
Icing sugar to dust

Grease and baseline a 21–23cm spring release tin. Cream together the butter and sugar until very pale. Gradually beat in the eggs – adding a little flour if the mixture curdles. Gently stir into the mixture the flour, ground almonds & almond essence.
Roll out the marzipan so it is just slightly bigger than the cake tin. Cut into a circle using the tin as a template.
Place half the cake mixture in the tin and shake level. Cover with the circle of marzipan and then top with the rest of the cake mixture.
Bake at 180°C / gas mark 4 for about 1¼ hours until firm to touch, covering with foil if necessary to stop it burning.
Leave to cool for 5 minutes before taking out of the tin. When completely cool, wrap in foil and leave for at least a day before serving.

Should be sticky in the middle!

Chocolate Raspberry Cake (KS)

Standard size (or large size in brackets)
175g plain chocolate (280g)
175g caster sugar (280g)
5 eggs (8), separated
1 punnet raspberries (2)
Thick cream, or double cream whipped until thickened

Preheat oven to 180°C / gas mark 4.
Line two 18cm (for larger cake, use 23cm) tins with a disc of greaseproof paper (put a little oil in the tin to stick it in). Melt the chocolate in a bowl over a pan of simmering water.
Whisk the egg yolks with the sugar using an electric whisk until light in colour and thickened. Whisk in the melted chocolate. Whisk in two (three) tablespoons of hot water to soften the mixture.
Whisk the eggs whites until they are stiff. Fold the eggs whites into the mixture. Pour into the tins and bake for 18–20 minutes (or 25 minutes if making the larger version). Allow to cool, then remove from the tins and chill in the fridge.

Assemble by putting a layer of cream and raspberries onto one half, then top with the other half. Put a doily on top of the cake then sprinkle icing sugar over it. Remove the doily to give a very pretty effect. If you don't eat it all in one sitting, this will keep in the fridge for a day or two.

Lemon Poppy Seed Muffins (CS)

250g plain flour
150g caster sugar
4 tbs poppy seeds
2 tsp baking powder
1 tsp bicarbonate of soda
½ tsp salt
2 eggs
250g lemon yoghurt
4 tbs vegetable oil
1 tbs grated lemon zest

For the drizzle
80ml lemon juice
3 tbs caster sugar

Preheat oven to 200°C / gas mark 6. Prepare a muffin tin (grease or line with paper cases).
Combine the flour, caster sugar, poppy seeds, baking powder, bicarbonate of soda and salt.
In a separate bowl mix the eggs, yoghurt, vegetable oil and lemon zest. Blend well and pour over the flour mixture. Mix until just combined – do not over-mix.
Spoon evenly between the prepared cases and pop into the oven for 20 minutes.

To make the drizzle: Combine the lemon juice and caster sugar and stir until the sugar dissolves. Once the muffins are baked, pierce the tops with a skewer. Slowly pour about one tablespoon of the drizzle mix over the top of each muffin.

Leave the muffins to cool for about 10 minutes before removing from the tin.

Chocolate Beetroot Muffins (CS)

You can freeze cooked, diced beetroot in plastic containers.
This is a great recipe to use up beetroot during the year.

60g cocoa powder
185g plain flour
2tsp baking powder
235g caster sugar
235g beetroot, cooked and peeled
3 large eggs
200ml corn oil
1tsp vanilla extract
Icing sugar for dusting (optional)

Preheat the oven to 180°C / 160°C fan / gas mark 4.
Line a 12-mould muffin tin with paper cases.
Sift the cocoa powder, flour and baking powder into a
bowl. Mix in the sugar and set aside.
Purée the beetroot in a food processor. Add the eggs, one
at a time, then add the oil and vanilla extract and blend
until smooth.Make a well in the centre of the dry
ingredients, add the beetroot mixture and mix lightly.
Divide the mixture between the 12 muffin cases. Bake for
20–30 minutes until the tops are firm when pressed and a
skewer inserted in the middle comes out clean.

Cool on a wire rack. Dust with icing sugar to serve if
desired.

JAMS, CHUTNEYS AND PRESERVES

Di's Orange Marmalade (PM)

This recipe comes from my stepmother-in-law, who makes pots and pots of delicious marmalade every January, and keeps the whole family supplied for the following year.

3kg Seville oranges
2 lemons, juice only
2 litres of water
2.6kg preserving or granulated sugar

Put the whole oranges and lemon juice in a large preserving pan and cover with 2 litres of water. Bring to the boil, cover and simmer very gently for about 2 hours, or until the peel can be easily pierced with a fork.
Warm half the sugar in an ovenproof bowl in a very low oven. Pour the cooking water from the oranges into a jug and tip the oranges into a bowl. Return the cooking liquid to the pan. Allow oranges to cool until they are easy to handle, then cut in half. Scoop out all the pips and pith and add to the reserved orange liquid in the pan. Bring to the boil and simmer for 6 minutes, then strain this liquid through a sieve into a bowl and press the pulp through with a wooden spoon – it is high in pectin so helps the marmalade to set.
Measure the liquid and pour half into a preserving pan. Cut the peel into fine shreds. Add half the peel to the liquid in the preserving pan with the warm sugar. Stir over a low heat until all the sugar has dissolved, (takes about 10

minutes), then bring to the boil and bubble rapidly for 15–25 minutes until setting point is reached.

Take the pan off the heat and skim any scum from the surface. Leave the marmalade to stand in the pan for about 20 minutes to cool a little and allow the peel to settle; then pot in sterilised jars, seal and label. Repeat with the remaining liquid, sugar and peel, remembering to warm the sugar first.

Rhubarb and Ginger Conserve (CS)

1.1kg rhubarb, trimmed, washed and cut into small pieces
1.1kg preserving sugar
25g fresh root ginger
100g stem ginger, roughly chopped

Put the rhubarb in a bowl in layers with the sugar, cover and leave overnight.

Put the rhubarb and sugar in a preserving pan. Crush or "bruise" the root ginger slightly with a rolling pin or hammer and tie in a piece of muslin. Add to the pan and bring slowly to the boil stirring until the sugar has dissolved. Boil rapidly for 15 minutes.

Add the stem ginger to the pan and boil for a further 5 minutes.

Remove the muslin bag and any scum with a slotted spoon, then pot in sterilised jars, and cover.

Beetroot Relish (CS)

My 102 year old grannie loves this. She eats it with spoon, straight from the jar. You wouldn't let children do that, but at 102 you can do whatever you want.

1.35kg beetroot, cooked and cut into small dice
450g shallots, finely chopped
600ml red wine vinegar
1 tbs pickling spice, placed in a muslin bag
450g granulated sugar

Put the shallots and vinegar in a preserving pan and cook for 10 minutes on a slow heat. Add the beetroot and muslin bag of pickling spice. Stir, add the sugar and cook gently until the sugar has dissolved. Bring to the boil and cook at a rolling boil for 5 minutes. Reduce the heat to a simmer and cook for about 40 minutes or until the mixture thickens. Remove the spice bag, then ladle the mixture into sterilized jars with non-metallic lids, making sure there are no air gaps. Seal, label and store in a cool, dark place. Allow the flavours to mature for 1 month and refrigerate after opening. Keeps for 9 months.

Spicy Plum Chutney (NR)

This chutney is delicious with cheese and also works as a sweet and spicy dip with poppadums or naan. Once opened it keeps about a month in the fridge.

1.5kg/3lb plums, stones removed
3 lemons, cut into small pieces, pips removed
3 lemons, juice only
1 tbs fresh ginger, peeled and grated
1 tbs cumin seeds
1 stick of cinnamon
½ tsp cayenne pepper
½ tsp garam masala
250ml/8fl oz water
200g/7oz brown sugar

Put everything except the sugar into a large, heavy-based pan. Heat it gently, stirring occasionally, until the plums soften and begin to disintegrate.
Stir in the sugar, then continue to cook it gently, testing now and again until the mixture is the consistency that you like. If you want to use it as a dip, you need to keep it fairly soft, so be careful not to overcook it. Remove the cinnamon stick and put the mixture into prepared, sterilised jam jars — it makes about 2 litres/3½ pints.

Mincemeat (NJ)

It is impossible for anyone to want shop-made mincemeat after one has made one's own; a child can do it, and there is nothing to cook.

225g apples (Bramleys are best)
50g suet
225g raisins
225g sultanas
225g currants
100g mixed candied orange, citron and lemon peel (optional)
100-125g blanched almonds (ie skins removed by immersion in boiling water for a few minutes)
Half a nutmeg, finely grated
125g Demerara sugar
½ tsp salt
½ tsp ground ginger
½ tsp ground cloves
½ tsp powdered cinnamon
½ tsp mixed spice
100-125ml rum, brandy or other spirit (I have used Pimms left from summer feasts)

Peel, core and grate the apples. Chop the almonds quite finely. Add the suet, chopping up if necessary. Add all the dry ingredients and mix really well with a wooden spoon. Leave overnight, then stir in rum, brandy or other spirit and bottle in clean, sterilised jars. Store in the fridge and use to fill mince pies. Can also be stored in plastic boxes in the freezer.

When you make your mince pies, add some orange juice and grated orange zest to the pastry mix, for extra tasty pies.

Aubergine and Apple Chutney (CS)

350g aubergines, roughly chopped
450g tomatoes, skinned and chopped
225g cooking apples, peeled, cored and sliced
175g onion, skinned and chopped
1 garlic clove, skinned and crushed
175g dark brown soft sugar
1 level tsp salt
300ml distilled vinegar
2 level tsp whole pickling spices

Place the aubergines, tomatoes, apples, onion and garlic in a preserving pan (or large, heavy-based saucepan) and add the brown sugar, salt and vinegar.Tie the pickling spices in a piece of muslin and add to the pan.

Bring to the boil then simmer uncovered, stirring occasionally, for about one hour or until the ingredients are soft and the contents of the pan well reduced.

Remove the bag of spices. Spoon the chutney into prepared sterilised jars, cover and seal.

Apricot and Orange Marmalade (CS)

2 Seville oranges, washed and quartered
1 lemon, washed and quartered
1.2 litres water
900g apricots, stoned and thinly sliced
900g granulated sugar

Remove the pips from the citrus fruits and tie them in a muslin bag. Finely chop the oranges and lemon in a food processor and put in a preserving pan with the muslin bag of pips and the water. Bring to the boil, then simmer, covered, for 1 hour.
Add the apricots to the pan, return to the boil then simmer for 30–40 minutes or until the fruits are very tender.
Remove the muslin bag. Add the sugar to the pan and stir over a low heat until the sugar has dissolved. Bring to the boil then boil rapidly for 15 minutes, stirring occasionally, until setting point (105°C) is reached.
Remove the pan from the heat and skim off any scum from the surface using a slotted spoon. Leave to cool for about five minutes, then stir and pour into warmed sterilised jars. Seal, then label when cold.

Note: It is important to use a food processor to chop the oranges and lemon. Chopping them this finely gives the marmalade its wonderful consistency. Preparing the fruit by hand will not give the same result.

Damson Jam (JJ)

1kg damsons
1.25kg preserving (or granulated) sugar
400ml water

Put the fruit and water in a big pan and simmer until the skins are soft and the fruit has reduced by a third. Take the pan off the heat and add the sugar, stirring gently until it is all dissolved.
When the sugar is completely dissolved return it to the heat and boil rapidly until setting point is reached. Take off the heat and let it sit for about 15 minutes to cool slightly. Skim off any scum and pot into sterilised jars.
Makes about six pots.

Note: as the stones are left in, please be careful when eating, as they can damage teeth!

Piccalilli (NC)

225g (8oz) salt
450g (1lb) pickling onions
1 medium cauliflower broken into small florets
225g (8oz) runner beans sliced into 1cm lengths
2 cucumbers or courgettes diced into 1cm cubes
2 heads of plump garlic

Pour 450ml (15 fl oz) boiling water over the salt in a large
bowl and stir to dissolve. Add a further 1.7 litres (3 pints)
cold water. Add the prepared vegetables and leave to soak
overnight.

Sauce
30g (1oz) plain flour
60g (2oz) mustard powder
225g (8oz) white sugar
1 tbsp ground turmeric
750ml (1¼ pints) distilled malt vinegar

Combine the flour, mustard powder, sugar and turmeric in
a large bowl. Add a little of the vinegar to make a smooth
paste. Mix in the remaining vinegar and tip it into a large
preserving pan and bring to the boil, whisking constantly.
Simmer for 4–5 minutes until the sauce is thick and
smooth.
Drain and rinse the vegetables and add to the sauce.
Simmer for 3 minutes or so until the veg are cooked but

still crisp. Pot into hot sterilised jars, pressing down the vegetables to ensure they are covered by the sauce. Seal with vinegar proof lids and label.
Makes 2kg and keeps for 6 months. Once opened, keep in the fridge.

Rhubarb and Date Chutney (CS)

500g red onions, chopped
50g fresh root ginger, grated
300ml red wine vinegar
500g eating apples, peeled and finely chopped
200g pitted dates, chopped
200g dried cranberries
1 tbs mustard seeds
1 tbs curry powder
400g light muscovado sugar
700g rhubarb, sliced into 2cm chunks

Put the onions in a preserving pan with the ginger and vinegar. Bring to the boil then simmer for 10 minutes.
Add the rest of the ingredients, except the rhubarb, to the pan and return to the boil, stirring. Simmer, uncovered, for about 10 minutes or until the apples are tender.
Stir in the rhubarb and cook, uncovered, until the chutney is thick and jammy (about 10–15 minutes).
Spoon into sterilised jars and seal. Label the jars when cool. Keep for at least a month before eating.

DRINKS

Plum Brandy (NC)

We usually have a glut from our Victoria plum tree on the allotment, and end up making endless crumbles, chutneys and sauces, however this is one of the nicest ways to use them up.

1kg plums
750g sugar
1 litre brandy

Wash and dry the plums. Pop them into a 2 litre Kilner-type jar, with a lid that seals. Pour in the brandy, then add the sugar. Gently shake the jar and pop it somewhere visible, so you don't forget about it.
For the next week or so shake the jar each day until the sugar is dissolved, then put it in a cupboard for at least 2 months.
Then decant the liquid into a sterilised bottle and leave it for as long as you can. It's delicious after about 6 months. If you leave it much longer the plums may break up and you get bits of plum floating in the brandy. If this happens, just strain the brandy through a clean piece of muslin when you decant it.

Delicious Blackberry Liqueur (DE)

Blackberries from my allotment
Granulated sugar
Whisky
A large screw top jar

Put ripe blackberries into a large screw-top jar, until it is
three quarters full. Fill to the top with granulated sugar.
Pour in whisky (needn't be the most expensive brand –
supermarket is fine) up to the top.
Screw the lid on and leave for 6 months. Strain and put into
a bottle – or you can just leave it in the jar and take out
liqueur when needed.

Elderflower Champagne (KS)

4 large heads of elderflower (at least, I always use more)
Rind and juice of a lemon
3 tbs of white wine vinegar
750g (1½lb) sugar
5 litres (1 gallon) water

Also needed: 5 strong litre bottles, sterilised
              A funnel
              Muslin to strain through

Put all the ingredients in a clean bucket, stir well, cover and leave for 24 hours.
Pick out the elderflower heads. Strain the remainder through muslin and pour a jug full at a time through muslin into strong clean screw top bottles with the help of a funnel. Leave in a cool place for at least 2 weeks before drinking.

Note: This amazing drink will keep for up to a year (but not if your family and friends know you have made it!). If you manage to keep it away from would be drinkers for any length of time, you must release the pressure (gently) on a regular basis, by opening the screw top a little now and again.

Elderflower Cordial (DR)

1k sugar
1.5 litres boiling water
4 medium lemons, washed to remove wax (or use unwaxed)
30 large elderflower heads, shaken to remove any insects
55g citric acid

Also needed: Sterilised 2 litre bottle, a funnel and a piece of muslin to strain the liquid through

Put the sugar into a large saucepan or a large heatproof bowl. Pour in the boiling water stir until all the sugar has dissolved. Leave to cool.
Grate the zest of the lemons with a fine grater, and add to the sugar water. Slice the lemons into thick slices and add to the water. Add the citric acid and stir, then finally add the flower heads to the water and stir again.
Cover with a clean cloth and leave to steep for 48 hours. Strain the liquid through clean fine muslin cloth into a clean bowl. Using a funnel, fill a sterilised bottle. Seal and store in a cool, dark place (but not the refrigerator) for a few weeks or you can freeze it in a plastic bottle in which case it will keep for longer.
This cordial is delicious diluted with still or fizzy water or used as a flavouring with ice cream and other fruity desserts. Once the bottle is opened, store it in the refrigerator.

Mulled Wine (JJ)

2 oranges, unwaxed
1 lemon, unwaxed, peel only
150g caster sugar
5 cloves, plus extra for garnish
5 cardamom pods, bruised
1 cinnamon stick
Pinch freshly grated nutmeg
2 bottles fruity, un-oaked red wine
150ml ginger wine

Peel and juice 1 orange, and add to a large saucepan along with the lemon peel, sugar and spices. Add enough wine to just cover the sugar, and heat gently until the sugar has dissolved, stirring occasionally.
Bring to the boil and cook for 5–8 minutes until you have a thick syrup.
Meanwhile, if you're serving it immediately, stud the second orange with 6 vertical lines of cloves, then cut into segments to use as a garnish.
Turn the heat down and pour the rest of the wine into the saucepan, along with the ginger wine. Gently heat through and serve with the orange segments as a
garnish. Alternatively, you can allow the syrup to cool and pour it into sterilised bottles for use later.

Fresh Lemonade (DeE)

6 large lemons (preferable unwaxed)
150g granulated sugar
2½ pints boiling water

Scrub the lemons if necessary in warm water to remove any wax, then thinly peel off the outer coloured zest from 3 of them using a zester or sharp potato peeler. Remove any white pith from the zest using a sharp knife, as it might make the lemonade bitter. Put the zest into a large bowl, with the juice from all 6 lemons.
Stir in the sugar, the pour in the boiling water. Stir it well, then cover the bowl and leave overnight in a cool place, (but not the fridge). The following day, stir again and taste to check for sweetness. You may need to add a bit more sugar. If it tastes fine, strain it through a sieve into sterilized bottles, top them and chill in the fridge. You can drink this straight, or diluted with still or sparkling water. Also delicious with soda water.

Makes about 3 pints.

Sloe Gin (DeE)

450g sloes, washed
225g caster sugar
1 litre gin

Prick the skins of the sloes all over with a thick needle, then
put them into a large sterilized jar.
Tip in the sugar, then add the gin, seal the lid and shake it
well. Put the jar into a cool, dark cupboard and every day,
give it a good shake, every day for the first week, then
about once a week for a couple of months.
After two or three months, strain the liquor through fine
muslin into a sterilised bottle.

Home Made Ginger Beer (NR)

140g fresh ginger, peeled
4 tbs dark brown sugar (preferably muscovado)
2 or 3 lemons (according to taste)
1 litre of soda water or sparkling mineral water
A few sprigs of fresh mint to serve

Grate the ginger on a coarse cheese grater and put the ginger together with any juice into a bowl. Sprinkle with the brown sugar.
Thinly remove the zest from 2 of the lemons using a sharp knife or potato peeler, add to the bowl, and mix the zest up with the ginger and sugar. Squeeze the juice from all 3 lemons, keeping just a little of the juice back.
Pour in the water and allow to sit for about 10 minutes, then taste. If it seems a bit sour, add a bit more sugar, if it's a bit sweet add the reserved lemon juice. Pour the ginger beer through a sieve into a large jug and serve with ice and a sprig of mint.

Index to Recipes